I0796195

Milan

past | present | future

Chiara Dal Canto

Milan

past | present | future

photographs by Lea Anouchinsky

New York Paris London Milan

A VITTORIO EMANUE
DUOMO 21
DUOMO 21

I MILANESI
APEROL
TERRAZZA
APEROL
TERRAZZA

There is one marvel in Milan, and undoubtedly the greatest, which I cannot leave unnoted—it is the Cathedral. From a distance it looks as though cut from white notepaper, and when near it the observer is startled to find that this lace-like scissoring is all of white marble. If we study the entire work a while longer, we find that it is right pretty, colossally neat, a play thing for giant children. But it appears best in the midnight moonshine, for then all the white stone men come thronging solemnly down from their heights and whisper an old legend in our ear.

Heinrich Heine, Pictures of Travel, 1830

FUTUR
LIBER
TY
AVANGUARDIA E STILE
MUSEO DEL NOVECENTO

Contents

Blue Label
TALISKER
PATRÓN
GRAN PATRÓN
PATRÓN EL CIELO
PATRÓN
PATRÓN
WHISTLEPIG
WHISTLEPIG
12
OLD WORLD RYE
WHISTLEPIG
SMALL BATCH RYE
10
GIN MARE
HENDRICK'S
HENDRICK'S
HENDRICK'S
PATRÓN
PATRÓN
1942

INTRODUCTION

It used to be just a city of work—austere, efficient, busy to the point of obsession. A pragmatic city, dedicated to doing and, it must be acknowledged, to "doing well." It was not a place people visited for vacations or tourism, but rather for professional engagements. Over time, the title bestowed upon it —"capital of the Italian economic miracle"—enhanced its dynamic and productive image even more.

A black-and-white city, considered not to be beautiful. A masculine city, unlike other Italian cities, all of which are feminine, as described in his imaginative and cultured prose by Gianni Brera, a journalist and writer deeply immersed in the culture of the Po Valley. Speaking of the Lombard capital, he wrote: "Milan has its own character: it produces, it does not contemplate, and even less so does it regret." And retracing its history with a well-recognized practical sense, he added: "The number of times Milan has been destroyed has been lost to history and arithmetic—but if we have always rebuilt it, then it must have been worth it."

Foggy Milan (now less so than in the past), softened by a light, woolly haze, immersed in a grayness not devoid of poetry, has inspired numerous artists. It has fueled the imagination of filmmakers and writers who have chosen it as an object of observation, making it the backdrop for suburban stories—like Luchino Visconti in *Rocco and His Brothers*—or of rebellion, like *It's a Hard Life*, by the Tuscan writer Luciano Bianciardi.

Even today, Milan is a city that never stops. It looks ahead with the determination to shape its future, envisioning itself as one of the most appealing destinations not only for tourism but also for business opportunities, investments, culture, and networking.

This dynamism is evocatively reflected in its concentric layout, forming a sequence of expanding circles radiating outward from its heart—the Duomo, the symbol of the city *par excellence*. It took over four hundred years to build, relying on a dedicated construction factory with its own quarries, which supplied the Candoglia marble transported along the waterways.

It can certainly be said that in the new millennium, Milan has shed its traditionally stern and duty-bound image to become not only the capital of fashion and design, but also a hub of ideas, capable of realizing internationally significant projects.

We could say that Milan has become less "Milanese"—more cosmopolitan, thanks to the many foreigners who have chosen to live here, often for professional reasons, and to the numerous visitors who come for culture, shopping, or study.

Milanese style has become a point of attraction for many tourists. Without losing its pragmatism, the city has embraced high-end hospitality, where the pleasures of fine dining and cultural experiences satisfy even the most discerning of palates.

As a result, historic residences belonging to noble dynasties and former religious buildings have been converted into luxury hotels. A distinguished traveler like Stendhal had good reason, during his stays in Milan, to lavish passionate praise on its palaces and monuments. "I entered a magnificent courtyard," he wrote, "climbed a superb staircase [...] and soon I found myself in a splendid hall. I was captivated, and, for the first time, I felt the true importance of architecture." This revelation was followed by his enthusiastic praise for "certain exquisite breaded cutlets. For many years, this dish continued to remind me of Milan," he admitted.

Milan's rich culinary tradition remains deeply rooted in its history, but like all great metropolises, it has embraced international influences to the point that today the city has truly become a gourmand destination. And, as locals proudly claim, only in Milan can you find the freshest fish in all of Italy.

Milan is a cultured city. This is proven by the presence of a temple of music like La Scala, its historic libraries, and its numerous museums. Visiting Milan means traveling through history, tracing remnants of Roman, medieval, Renaissance, Enlightenment, Napoleonic, Habsburg, Risorgimento, and industrial eras.

Despite its natural inclination toward understatement, Milan can claim a rich twentieth-century artistic heritage, one that resonates in the present and extends far beyond national borders. Lucio Fontana, Piero Manzoni, and Fausto Melotti are just a few of the artists who worked in the city and whom Milan today celebrates. One could even say that, thanks to the appreciation and recognition of foreign visitors, Milan has rediscovered its own architecture. The buildings designed by Gio Ponti, Piero Portaluppi, or Luigi Caccia Dominioni serve as landmarks, offering a way to reinterpret the history of the twentieth century—not just the city's stylistic evolution but also and above all its social history.

One of Milan's most beloved symbols, the Torre Velasca—designed by the BBPR Studio and inaugurated in 1961—features a complex aesthetic that blends Brutalism with references to medieval Lombard architecture. Initially, it was not to everyone's liking, perhaps because its boldness was considered excessive. Today, however, it is an admired and studied building, drawing the attention of students and tourists alike.

When it comes to contemporary architecture, one cannot fail to mention the Bosco Verticale by Boeri Studio, which has become an international icon to the point of being reproduced in other countries. Milan's skyline itself has dramatically changed over the past two decades, with radical transformations that have given it a more global profile. This is clear to see in such striking buildings as the Fondazione Feltrinelli, by the architects Herzog & de Meuron, or the new Bocconi University Campus, by Studio SANAA.

Fashion and design are the pillars upon which Milan has built its identity. Though distinct in terms of history and evolution, and shaped by different key figures, these two disciplines have worked in synergy to make the city a global hub of creativity at the highest levels.

Fashion in Milan took off in the 1970s, owing to a group of designers who didn't just innovate but revolutionized the industry, experimenting with new aesthetics and achieving unprecedented success.

Their work thrived thanks to the collaboration with the worlds of communication and publishing, with visual creatives, and marketing experts who found fertile ground in Milan.

Design, on the other hand, has a longer history, born from the extraordinary fusion of craftsmanship and industry, the dialogue between visionary designers and enlightened entrepreneurs, the discovery of new materials, the evolution of domestic living, and the imperative to make what is functional also beautiful.

We have chosen to tell the story of fashion through one of its leading figures: Giorgio Armani, the undisputed master of precision and elegance. As for design, it could only be represented by the institution that has symbolized it from the very beginning: the Triennale. Inaugurated in 1933 in the Palazzo dell'Arte, designed by Giovanni Muzio, it has played a pivotal role in promoting, sharing, and fostering international dialogue in the field of design.

This book is not meant to be a city guide. Rather, it aims to spark curiosity in those who are unfamiliar with Milan, evoke memories in those who have visited, and offer a fresh perspective on some of its most well-known subjects.

Lea Anouchinsky's photographs capture the city at dawn, before it has fully stirred from its slumber—when the sounds are muffled and the tourists have yet to emerge. It is in this moment that Milan's architecture becomes most expressive, its spaces more legible, and one's gaze can rise upward to discover unusual, unseen perspectives.

Because Milan still manages to surprise even its own residents. And although it is flat, without the sea and always on the move, it has learned to enjoy itself.

Chiara Dal Canto

DUOMO

GALLERIA VITTORIO EMANUELE II

CASA DEGLI OMENONI

PALAZZO BROGGI

PALAZZO CRESPI

TEATRO ALLA SCALA

PIAZZA BELGIOIOSO

A Concentric City

Some, like the painter and writer Dino Buzzati, have imagined it to be a mountain, a sort of Dolomitic ruin, owing to the complexity of its pinnacles and stone spires. Over time, Milan's Duomo has suggested numerous visions: a building symbolizing the city, a hub from which the road network radiates.

A never-ending worksite, over three thousand statues, and a facade that was completed following an order issued by Napoleon, who was crowned here in 1805. For years, the gilded Madonnina that sits atop it was not just a spiritual symbol but also the highest point in Milan, which no new building could surpass.

Monumentality is what characterizes the city's central core, starting from the buildings around the Duomo, first and foremost the Galleria Vittorio Emanuele II, the expression of nineteenth-century architectural culture, with its iron and glass roof. A path that connects the Cathedral to the nearby Piazza della Scala, a meeting-place for the bourgeoisie, the "salon" of the Milanese, an international window for shopping, the Galleria tells the story of a city that is proud of its past and ready to meet the present.

Monumental are the buildings inspired by neoclassicism that design the elliptical Piazza Cordusio, where business was done. While it once hosted the headquarters of banks, insurance companies, and financial institutions, it is mostly commercial now. The many private buildings are also monumental, including the one that bears the name of an entrepreneurial Milanese dynasty, that of the Crespi, engaged in the textile and electrical industries and co-owner of the newspaper *Corriere della Sera*. The project, commissioned from the architect Piero Portaluppi in the 1930s, features an array of decorative elements: marble of various colors, broken pediments, moldings, niches, and pilaster strips, without forsaking a precise sense of order. Lastly, there are the monumental figures known as the "Omenoni" ("Big Men"), adorning the facade of Palazzo Leoni-Calchi. Since the mid-sixteenth century, with their heads bowed and downward looking gaze, these stone giants are a reminder of their incarceration.

DUOMO

Its origins are uncertain, but the records testifying to its foundation date to the late fourteenth century. The project involved the alternating of French and German architects alongside Lombard and Tuscan masters. A Gothic masterpiece, from its origins to 1920 it has witnessed the arrival of the marble for its construction, over 550,000 blocks, along the course of the Navigli. More than three thousand statues decorate the exterior and interior, and the glasswork made using enamel-painted glass is notable. The gilded Madonnina has been one of Milan's most famous symbols since 1774. The terraces on the roof, a must-see, offer a panoramic view of the city.

APEROL
APEROL
APEROL

GALLERIA VITTORIO EMANUELE II

In 1863, the architect Giuseppe Mengoni won the competition to renovate Piazza del Duomo. The covered passage—connecting the Piazza *par excellence* to Piazza della Scala—opens up at the center to form an octagon topped by an iron and glass dome. The Galleria was created so that the people of Milan could meet in a place that was well-lit as well as being covered. Outside, high up, an open-air walkway runs all along the Galleria.

MARTINI

CASA DEGLI OMENONI

A synonym for "Omaccioni" ("Big Men"), also referred to as Telamons, the purpose of these male sculptures is to support architectural elements, functionally or decoratively. Made by Antonio Abbondio, they have decorated the facade of what was the residence of the sculptor and collector Leone Leoni since the sixteenth century, the silent witnesses of a city that has inexorably transformed.

STARBUCKS

PALAZZO BROGGI

Built between 1899 and 1901 and named after its architect, Palazzo Broggi housed the Stock Exchange and later the Post Office. With its slightly concave base, it contributes to the elliptical shape of Piazza Cordusio.

Renowned for their role in the textile industry and as co-owners of *Corriere della Sera*, the Crespi family entrusted architect Piero Portaluppi to design their residence. Completed in 1932, Palazzo Crespi stands at the intersection of Via Verri, Piazza Meda, and today's Corso Matteotti. Portaluppi captured upper-middle-class taste with refined classicism and elegant details, like the lozenge ceiling of the side porticoes of the Palazzo.

PALAZZO CRESPI

TEATRO ALLA SCALA

The facade of the Teatro alla Scala and, behind it, the cylindrical volume created when the theater was remodeled in the early 2000s by Mario Botta.

PIAZZA BELGIOIOSO

One of the city's most beautiful corners, surrounded by the neoclassical palazzo that gives its name to the square and by the residence of the great Italian writer Alessandro Manzoni, currently a museum. Here it is seen at daybreak, before the city awakens, and you can almost hear the sounds of the carriages that crossed it in the nineteenth century.

CASA CIPRIANI

TRATTORIA DEL CIUMBIA

IL SALUMAIO DI MONTENAPOLEONE

MANDARIN ORIENTAL HOTEL

LANGOSTERIA

Gourmet Luxury

Those who come to Milan imagining it to be provincial as compared with the world's other major cities, will soon change their minds. While Milan doesn't stretch out as much, making it fairly easy to get around, it does boast a well-organized transportation system, and believes in efficiency and doing things properly. It is also a city that offers gastronomic pleasures: the dining is good here, in excellent settings, and is usually accompanied by top-notch service.
There's a dress code that's not too formal, but, as the city is also the capital of the fashion world, a certain elegance comes naturally. One can choose between a place like the Trattoria del Ciumbia, that has echoes of the old traditional eateries, as reimagined by the glamorous interior design duo Dimorestudio; or a restaurant that has built up a solid reputation as concerns the quality of its dishes, especially the fish courses, called Langosteria.

The latter is so successful it has also been exported abroad, to Paris and Saint-Moritz.
As for hospitality, places like Casa Cipriani offer the exclusiveness of a club, spaces that have the warmth and the privacy of a discreet world, along with a great international tradition. At the Mandarin Oriental, Milan, a suite signed Fornasetti offers the chance to get acquainted with a brand born from an ingenious figure, with a fertile imagination, who succeeded in creating a very personal domestic universe. A designer, painter, and printer, Piero Fornasetti was at the heart of the Milanese culture of decoration in the twentieth century.
A methodical eccentric, a collector of motifs from zoology and botany, and from popular culture, among others, his unmistakable style left a mark on furniture and objects.

CASA CIPRIANI

In the historical spaces of Palazzo Bernasconi Casa Cipriani was born, a private club that bears the name of the family that made Harry's Bar famous in Venice. The welcome there is the kind you would receive in a private home, where the guests can move about freely between the four floors. There they will find two different restaurants, a spa, and a lounge. Thirteen rooms and two suites are also open to nonmembers. The interiors were designed by the famous Florentine architect Michele Bönan. Above, a corner of the restaurant; opposite, the Living Room on the top floor.

Opposite, the entrance to Casa Cipriani, where the original architectural elements stand out. Above, the Living Room, a lounge on the top floor, with live entertainment and a DJ mixset, the perfect venue for cocktails and music.

Opposite, the restaurant terrace with a view of the Indro Montanelli Public Gardens. Above, the rooms reveal their timeless elegance in the oakwood floors and the walnut boiserie, along with wallpaper in shades of blue and the marble bathroom.

Above and opposite, the Pickering Room on the ground floor, an elegant space for breakfast, lunch, dinner, or just a drink. Typical Italian dishes are served in addition to the traditional Cipriani fare.

TRATTORIA DEL CIUMBIA

In Milanese, the expression "Ciumbia" indicates wonder and awe. And the Disco Club located on the lower floor of the trattoria is truly awesome. "I was inspired by the 1980s, a decade that defined the night-time scene in Milan between boldness and sharp geometries," says Emiliano Salci,

founder of Dimorestudio together with Britt Moran. "I tried to recreate the same vibrant atmosphere, with a contemporary eye. Dynamic lights, contrasting colors, and reflecting material for a sensory experience, while the electronic music, with its hypnotic vibrations, is the throbbing heart."

Wooden boiserie tinted red and a multicolor floor in a trattoria that recalls the seventies mood, when Brera was the favorite neighborhood of the avant-garde artists.

In the traditional Lombard menu, *mondeghili* (meatballs), opposite, and *vitello tonnato* "revisited" are a must.

IL SALUMAIO DI MONTENAPOLEONE

The location is special: in the heart of the city, away from the traffic, in the courtyard and on the ground floor of the historical Palazzo Bagatti Valsecchi, which hosts the eponymous museum. A family business—whose windows at one time overlooked Via Montenapoleone—which for three generations has offered its famous gastronomy, a bistrot café, and a restaurant with a mouthwatering Mediterranean menu.

a Milano dal 1957
il Salumaio di Montenapoleone

MANDARIN ORIENTAL HOTEL

The Speciality Suite is a full immersion in Milano-ness, thanks to the total look created by the works of Piero Fornasetti, an original nonconformist who burst onto the scene of the twentieth century. His decorative themes, whether high or belonging to the popular culture, have "tattooed" furnishings, rugs, plates, textiles, and wallpaper.

A world that his son Barnaba, the artistic director of the atelier, inherited and made his own. His collaboration with the ACPV Architects firm of Antonio Citterio and Patricia Viel led to the creation of this suite, over 1,000 square feet of surface area covering the living area, bedroom, master bathroom, and guest bathroom. Butterflies, Palladian themes, clouds, capitals, and musical instruments create an atmosphere where the free imagination is combined with a clear sense of elegance.

Opposite, the hallway leading to the bedroom. In the dining area, above, a collection of assorted mirrors faces the pillar lined with Riflesso wallpaper.

In the king-size room, a writing desk of the Farfalle collection. Opposite, from the hourglass to the chessboard, a variation of themes both classical and humorous.

La contesa
è
il sale della

LANGOSTERIA

Founded in 2007, it became an international brand when it opened in Paris and Saint-Moritz, and with other international destinations planned. The ideas were clear from the day it opened: a menu of only fish, with a large selection of raw dishes. Tradition here alternates with ever-changing novelties: the specials of the day and signature dishes keep the menu up-to-date.

Opposite and above, the spaces of what can be considered the flagship restaurant, the first location that then was followed by a series of venues, all of which showcase a seafood-based gastronomy.

Above, left, a classic with a new touch: “Incorrect” ceviche of black grouper, referring to a new way of conceiving the marinade that brings out the flavor; right, grilled Huelva royal langoustines from the Gibraltar Strait and cooked on the “robata” of Italian beech charcoal, with no toxic elements. Opposite, one can sit at the counter or in the private dining room. There is a large selection of wines.

Opposite, a dimly-lit, intimate table. Above, the signature dish of the resaturant is King Crab 2007: in the Special Edition version, seven ingredients, one of which is secret, make for an exclusive sauce.

CAMPUS SDA BOCCONI
MUDEC
PORTA NUOVA
FONDAZIONE FELTRINELLI
PIRELLI HANGARBICOCCA
FONDAZIONE PRADA

A New Image

The ever-busy Milanese walk quickly and do not seem to pay much attention to art or to other intellectual concerns. But quite the opposite is true, as the city brims over with culture. Museums, institutions, libraries, foundations, universities: this city has it all. Culture is present here in its history and its traditions: in what have been acknowledged as “temples” of culture that celebrate it officially, in the less famous houses-cum-museums, and, lastly, in the former industrial buildings that are well suited to being repurposed into contemporary art exhibition venues.

Let’s not forget that in the eighteenth and nineteenth centuries Milan was a must-visit site for those on the Grand Tour who wanted to familiarize themselves with Italy’s art and culture. Once they had crossed the Alps, it was the first city where travelers would stop, given the importance of its artistic heritage. Moreover, unlike other capital cities in Italy, it was already a cosmopolitan, and not in the least provincial, place.

In addition to being a place of culture, Milan has many publishing houses. It is a city of businesspeople. It is the fashion capital of the

world. These factors led to the birth of the Fondazione Feltrinelli, whose headquarters is in a 650-foot-long bar-shaped building designed by the Swiss architectural firm Herzog & de Meuron; the Pirelli HangarBicocca, which transformed a workplace into a container where artworks converse with the surrounding space; the Fondazione Prada, which, thanks to its energy, has turned a previously neglected area of the city into a rather interesting one thanks to a project designed by Rem Koolhaas.
Architecture and education also produced the new Bocconi University Campus, featuring solutions with extraordinary visual effects, reminiscent, via circular constructions, of the gasometers that were once scattered across Milan's outskirts; these elements of the urban landscape were celebrated by the painter Mario Sironi in the mid-twentieth century. Another foreigner, the English architect David Chipperfield, left his mark on Milan's MUDEC-Museo delle Culture, in an area of the city that once produced consumer goods and now produces ideas instead.

CAMPUS SDA BOCCONI

Outside the center of the city, next to the original site of the University, the Campus SDA Bocconi was born. It is a complex that occupies a large area and that, thanks to the Japanese firm SANAA, has brought a sophisticated lightness to the architectural panorama of the city. The campus consists of cylindrical buildings of different heights that are luminous thanks to the ample glazed portions. The buildings are wrapped in a silvery and wavy metal mesh that follows their circular shape, remaining detached from the structure and suspended from the ground. These transparent, organic forms surrounded by greenery fulfill the architects' desire to establish "a porous relationship with the city."

Classrooms, offices, residences, and a large sports center are the functions carried out by the high-sustainability structures. “Each building has an inner courtyard that is typical of Milanese tradition,” the architects explain, “and each has its own character within a larger system.” Openness and transparency express an architectural concept that is rather different from the one that, in the late 1930s, inspired the first site of Bocconi, today one of the most prestigious universities in the world. Above, a view of the sky between the buildings of the historic headquarters.

MUDEC

The Museo delle Culture was created on the occasion of the International Expo in 2015, which gave the city a strong growth incentive. Hosting the ethno-anthropological collections of the City of Milan are the spaces that once belonged to the Ansaldo steel plants. The British architect David Chipperfield was commissioned to remodel the building. He designed the glazed "cloud" that defines the central foyer and features an amoebic shape, a "lantern that serves as a light for the whole place," according to the architect. A courtyard inside a courtyard, a mellow and luminous presence in a system of rooms based on rigidity. MUDEC draws visitors who come to see its permanent collections, as well as the numerous temporary exhibitions that it hosts, devoted to art, photography, and installations, for an eclectic and lively calendar of events.

PORTA NUOVA

This is the new Milan, one of the areas where tall glass buildings have risen up, forming a break from the city's tradition and speaking an international language. The high-rises, more than twenty, have redesigned a hybrid area between the train station, tracks, and old constructions, thus creating the Management Center: commercial, cultural, and residential spaces that are in part distributed over a super-elevated pathway with respect to the street level. The tallest skyscraper, named Torre Unicredit, above and opposite, is the work of César Pelli and generated—thanks to its semicircular shape and with the completion of other buildings—Piazza Gae Aulenti. On the following pages are the Solaria and Solea towers.

FONDAZIONE FELTRINELLI

This highly prestigious cultural institution stands alongside the eponymous publishing house of great tradition: both of them bear the name of Giangiacomo Feltrinelli, who inspired them. The study center has a library, a rich archive, a reading room, a bookshop, and offices, and it promotes cultural initiatives in a calendar that is filled with events, debates, and meetings. The library alone has over 200,000 books and periodicals, including antique and rare works. The archive contains the numerous fonds of institutions and private families. These are safeguarded so that they can be consulted by students and scholars.

For several years now, Fondazione Feltrinelli has been housed in a prestigious complex designed by the Swiss architects Herzog & de Meuron, whose creation has become a landmark of the urban landscape. The inspiration is based on the building's location along a segment of the sixteenth-century Spanish city wall.
It is a massive structure, divided into two parts, with a strong visual impact that is solid and transparent at the same time, due to the large windows, and it is a strong bulwark in defense of culture, history, and memory.
Opposite, the stairs that climb from the rooms on the ground floor to the library under the sloping ceiling, shown on the following page. On page 99, the two identical buildings are clearly separated.

PIRELLI HANGARBICOCCA

The edifice bears witness to the transformation of an area used for building locomotives to a museum dedicated to contemporary art. The Pirelli company purchased the 160,000-square-foot hangar—an enormous space where the echo of machinery at work still seems to linger—and in 2004 transformed it into exhibition spaces for both Italian and international solo shows. Milan acquired Anselm Kiefer's must-see permanent installation *I Sette Palazzi Celesti* (2002–2015), opposite. Outside, the public is welcomed by Fausto Melotti's intallation *La Sequenza* (1971–1981), below.

FONDAZIONE PRADA

Collecting, patronage, art, archeology, musical events, performances, cinema, scientific meetings, and teaching activities: the Fondazione Prada is a multidisciplinary cultural institution that represented a real change for the city. Loved by the Milanese, it is a must-see for visitors.
In an area south of Milan that is definitely off the beaten track, the birth of the Fondazione drove the transformation of a neighborhood, where new construction stands side by side with the repurposing of industrial buildings.
The Fondazione as well is located in what was once a distillery, whose spaces were adapted to host exhibitions, with new spaces added in a project designed by the OMA firm, directed by Rem Koolhaas. The preexisting structure, called The Haunted House, covered in gold leaf, and the last building, called Torre, have become emblems of Milan.
In the Torre are located large-scale installations, as well as a restaurant with a panoramic terrace. The spaces all differ, aesthetically as well, and serve as a backdrop to exhibitions that are often surprising in terms of the theme and quality of the works.
Opposite, *Upside Down Mushroom Room*, 2000, by Carsten Höller, one of the installations that make up the Atlas project, which unfolds across several floors in the Torre.

A place that includes very different spaces, to be discovered along routes that visitors can choose freely. The new buildings, which include the Podium, the Cinema, and the Torre have been grafted onto preexisting constructions.

"Old and new, horizontal and vertical, narrow and wide, black and white, open and closed: these contrasts establish the variety of oppositions that describe the new Fondazione's nature," explains Rem Koolhaas.

Bar Luce is always crowded and has become an iconic place in which to meet, especially appreciated by those who love vintage revivals. It was designed by the filmmaker Wes Anderson, who conceived it as an authentic space as opposed to an artificial film set: "I tried to create a place where you could go five times a week," he remarked. "When I was a child, I wanted to be an architect, and that's why for me this was the perfect opportunity to pretend I really was one!"

The references are inspired by the old Milanese cafés of the 1950s and 1960s, colorful Formica for the furnishings, and tapestry for the ceiling and walls, reproducing the glass ceiling and the facade of the buildings of Galleria Vittorio Emanuele II.

BVLGARI HOTEL
DA GIACOMO
CAMPARINO IN GALLERIA
PORTRAIT MILANO
ARMANI HOTEL MILANO

Italian Delights

Refined suites, away from the hustle and bustle of the city and overlooking a private 43,000-square-foot garden—an extension of the Orto Botanico di Brera—are one of the reasons to stay at the Bvlgari Hotel Milano. Located in the heart of the city, just behind Via Brera and the Pinacoteca bearing the same name, the hotel provides a stunning view of a vast green area. This is Milan: austere facades that conceal pleasant surprises, courtyards designed with architectural precision, and series of columns that boast a certain monumentality. Like those that outline the grand courtyard facing the Portrait Milano hotel, housed in a seventeenth-century building that once served as the Archiepiscopal Seminary. "This place is a treasure that few Milanese know about," said Michele De Lucchi, the architect behind the building's restoration project. In Milan, tradition matters.

The eagerness to innovate and the audacity of the most contemporary constructions do not replace old habits. Like enjoying an aperitif at Camparino in Galleria, which first opened in 1867. Galleria Vittorio Emanuele II had just been completed when this Liberty-style venue was built, right on the corner of Piazza del Duomo. Highly skilled artisans worked on it, and their craftsmanship can still be admired today while sipping a cocktail. Da Giacomo is another restaurant where history is palpable, from the names of its illustrious clientele—prominent figures in politics, entertainment, and the arts—to its design and decoration, the work of Renzo Mongiardino. Undoubtedly an unconventional architect, Mongiardino rejected the novelties of a certain modernism, and instead looked back to a past consisting of atmosphere, scenic compositions, and meticulously curated details.

BVLGARI HOTEL

Guests who choose to stay at the Bvlgari Hotel Milano are looking for discretion. Located at the end of a private street, the building, in the heart of the city, overlooks a very peaceful space. A before-dinner drink or an afternoon tea in the garden designed by the Swiss landscape artist Sophie Agata Ambroise, a dinner based on the suggestions of the multi-starred chef Niko Romito, a pause in the spa for a personalized treatment are just some of the rites that fill each guest's day. All of this in a very elegant setting, characterized by a contemporary style, thanks to APCV Architects, Antonio Citterio and Patricia Viel, masters of design and architecture.

DA GIACOMO

A great classic, with an old-fashioned atmosphere created by its decor and a menu mostly dedicated to fish, Da Giacomo (its founder was Giacomo Bulleri, described by the *New York Times* as "The man who cooked for Italy") has always had a local as well as a foreign clientele—including Maria Callas, Michelle Obama, and Lady Gaga—who could probably feel the *air du temps* of the early twentieth century here.
It was furnished by Renzo Mongiardino, an architect for the international bourgeoisie, who fell into oblivion in a city where design rules. He then returned to being sought after, as it happened here, in the rooms of Da Giacomo.
Opposite, the restaurant's interpretation of raw fish.

Boiserie, pastel hues, and the spirit of a simple and charming trattoria.

Unchanged over time, ever since Giacomo Bulleri came here in the 1990s.

CAMPARINO IN GALLERIA

This eatery is a must for a drink, lunch, or a coffee on the run. Its history began in 1867, when Gaspare Campari, the inventor of the eponymous bitter apéritif, opened Caffè Campari in Galleria Vittorio Emanuele II. Forty-eight years later, his son Davide inaugurated Camparino in Galleria. The Liberty-style interiors, opposite, are the work of the renowned cabinetmaker Eugenio Quarti, the master ironworker Alessandro Mazzucotelli, and the painter Angelo d'Andrea. In 2018, the venue was restyled by Lissoni Associati: in the Sala Spiritello, on the second floor, with a large counter covered in mirrors under a glass ceiling, above.
On the following pages, a view of the Galleria from the large arched windows.

PORTRAIT MILANO

One of the most recent additions to the Lombard metropolis, the hotel has become a cult venue thanks to its exceptional position in the very heart of the city. A little-known corner that once hosted the Seminario Arcivescovile, it has undergone a conservative refurbishment by the architect Michele De Lucchi. The palazzo embraces a seventeenth-century colonnade that has found a new life amid luxury and comfort.

Below, the glass gallery on the second floor, overlooked by the suites and rooms, and the ground floor, opposite.

Extraordinary architecture that is now open to all is revealed upon entering the baroque door on Corso Venezia.

Rooms and suites designed by Michele Bönan seem to belong to a refined dwelling.

HOMES
FOR
OUR TIME

The Hotel has two restaurants, the 10_11, featuring a garden and overlooking the colonnade, and the Beefbar, opposite, with a meat-based international menu.

Tacos made with Kobe beef in a butter, avocado, and habanero sauce.

BNP PARIBAS

ARMANI HOTEL MILANO

There's a correspondence between the elegance that Giorgio Armani offers in his sartorial creations and that of the interiors that he invented over the course of time, whether they are houses, restaurants, or hotels bearing his name.
It is an aesthetic that comprises balance, measure, elegance, and the prevalence of natural tones. On the topmost floors of the 1930s building, where the Armani world is expressed through restaurants, flowers, books, desserts, and fashion, the Hotel is distinguished for its interpretation of luxury that is both relaxed and sophisticated. Opposite and above, the Signature Suite Cinema, equipped with a Movie Room.

In the spa, which offers a panoramic view of the city, relaxation and personalized treatments are available in addition to thermal baths, saunas, steam baths, and ice showers.

BOSCO VERTICALE
BIBLIOTECA DEGLI ALBERI
VILLA INVERNIZZI
ORTO BOTANICO DI BRERA
GIARDINI MONTANELLI

Shades of Green

Created in the past to guarantee ornamentation and leisure, today greenery is indispensable to help offset the effects of climate change. Under each of its forms, it represents an essential theme in major city planning, in the creation of parks, and in its interaction with architecture.

Its original purpose, a landscape that could offer moments of shared pleasure, has remained unchanged. This is proven by the success of one of the last public parks that was created in Milan, the Biblioteca degli Alberi, conceived by the Dutch firm Inside Outside Petra Blaisse for the neighborhood of Porta Nuova and surrounded by the new constructions of the Management Center.

The city's first gardens open to all the people of Milan were the Giardini di Porta Venezia, as they are usually called, although they were recently renamed after the renowned Italian journalist Indro Montanelli. Created in the late eighteenth century and inspired by English models, in time they have grown and been transformed into their current arrangement. They are one of the city's more pleasant and popular sites.

The difference between these two green areas bears witness to how solutions for landscapes and botanical choices have changed over the years: design and lawns today, rocaille and lakes in the past. Milan boasts the skyscraper that more than others has represented the challenge of green architecture: the Bosco Verticale, designed by Boeri Studio, which has achieved considerable international acclaim. Its capacity to reduce energy consumption, thanks to the intensive use of vegetation, accompanies other numerous advantages: from the protection of biodiversity to its function as a filter for particulates, not to mention the changing visual effects in every season. The demand for it to be replicated in other countries is proof of just how timely the idea for the building was.

Further proof of the city's historical interest in botany is the Orto Botanico di Brera, hidden away just a stone's throw from the Pinacoteca: the gardens date back to the late eighteenth century, following the transformation of what in the past were the monastic gardens, where the monks cultivated plants and meditated.

BOSCO VERTICALE

Eight hundred trees, 15,000 perennials and/or groundcover, 5,000 shrubs: in 32,000 square feet the Bosco Verticale includes vegetation that is equivalent to 215,000 square feet of woods. The two towers that compose it have become an unmissable stop for visitors to Milan who want to admire a much-photographed example of sustainable architecture and, with luck, watch the spectacle of the Flying Gardeners: like mountaineers suspended in the void, they descend from the rooftop to prune the plants that are painstakingly cared for.

BAM – BIBLIOTECA DEGLI ALBERI

This is a contemporary garden, in the way it was conceived and the type of activity it hosts. Branching out from a grid of pathways are green rooms, play areas, blooming meadows, tree-lined areas, irregularly-shaped fields, and vegetable gardens without fencing. Its geometric grid is especially legible from above, but little does it matter: what counts is the variety—there are over a hundred botanical species—and the opportunity to enjoy the changing of the seasons and the flowering. One can also have moments of relaxation, encounters, and picnics when it's warm. There are many organized activities, cultural ones as well, wellness sessions, performances, and workshops for adults and children.

VILLA INVERNIZZI

Beyond Villa Invernizzi's gates one can see a small colony of pink flamingoes in the garden, an unusual presence in the heart of the city.

ORTO BOTANICO DI BRERA

Open to the public for just over two decades, these botanical gardens date back to the fourteenth century, when they belonged to the Humiliati friars. In the second half of the eighteenth century, thanks to the Empress Maria Therese of Austria, the Brera area became a lively cultural hub that included the gardens. Medicinal plants and ones used for natural dyeing, tall trees, shrubs: more than a thousand species grow in this space, hidden between the buildings that conceal them, turning it into a secret treasure trove.

GIARDINI MONTANELLI

From the terrace of Casa Cipriani, the view embraces the city as it has developed over the course of time. The tops of the tall trees of the Giardini Montanelli stand out against the new Milanese skyline, characterized by the towers of Porta Nuova. In the foreground, the neo-Gothic-style building dating from the late nineteenth century houses the Museum of Natural History. Many species are present in the park, including firs, maples, Lebanon cedars, a long row of horse chestnuts, and a monumental specimen of metasequoia.

BNP PARIBAS

PALAZZO DELL'ARENGARIO
PALAZZO MONTEDORIA
GRATTACIELO PIRELLI
TORRE VELASCA
TORRE SNIA VISCOSA
PALAZZO MEZZANOTTE

Classic
Novecento
Style

Milan's Novecento consists of intersections, encounters, juxtapositions, and felicitous cross-pollinations. Much of Milan's architecture in Novecento style has involved architects and artists in a very close relationship. This is true of the facades of the Palazzo dell'Arengario, consisting of two twin buildings that define the southern side of Piazza del Duomo. A series of bas-reliefs made by Arturo Martini, a sculptor of international fame, decorate the bases with plant motifs. The project, signed by four architects including Piero Portaluppi and Giovanni Muzio, contributes to the monumentality of the square and sits opposite the more famous Galleria. And once again art, especially that of the twentieth century—with precious works including several masterpieces of Futurism—found hospitality in one of the two buildings, the seat of the Museo del Novecento.

Sculptural works also decorate Palazzo Mezzanotte, named after the architect who designed it, completed in 1932 to host the seat of the Borsa Valori (Stock Exchange), in Piazza degli Affari. Travertine sculptures by Leone Lodi and Geminiano Cibau are located on the facade, combining Rationalist elements and Classical architecture. The figures are impressive, not devoid of the rhetoric that is required to celebrate the "four allegorical elements" of economic wealth.

But what has especially drawn attention for over a decade is the work *L.O.V.E* (an acronym for the Italian words Libertà, Odio, Vendetta, Eternità—Liberty, Hatred, Revenge, Eternity), by the contemporary artist Maurizio Cattelan: set on a stone base is a gigantic marble hand with its middle finger pointing skyward and its other fingers cut off. That finger establishes a curious dialogue with the building that houses the Borsa, with the fascist period that witnessed its emergence, and with high finance. The Roman salute or a disrespectful gesture?
Gio Ponti as well, a prolific, brilliant, internationally acclaimed architect, had many friends and collaborators who were artists. His architecture initially had connection to the metaphysical painting of De Chirico and Carrà, and the use of color in his interiors is often rooted in painting; moreover, in some of his buildings, the materials are applied in a sculptural manner. Similarly, in the Montedoria complex of residences and offices, the ceramic tiles used on the facades were finished to achieve a conspicuously sculptural effect.
An original synthesis of art and architecture is embodied in the striking ear-shaped sculpture by Adolfo Wildt, which serves as an analog intercom on the façade of Palazzo Sola-Busca (1927), designed by Aldo Andreani. Milan owes much of its cultural prestige to the Novecento.

PALAZZO DELL'ARENGARIO

The main perspective of the great Piazza del Duomo faces the front of the church. All around, buildings from different eras make up the scenery of the quadrilateral, whose rhythm is in part set by the pattern of the porticoes. On the southern side are the two volumes of the Arengario, a term that once indicated the headquarters of the City Administration, clad in pink Candoglia marble, the same as the Duomo. Piero Portaluppi is its most famous architect, even though the team that won the competition to design it consisted of four architects. Built between 1937 and 1956, during the fascist period it was used as a stage for political events and was completed when the war ended. A recent competition chose a solution that imagines a walkway connecting the two buildings it is made up of.

The building next to Palazzo Reale hosts the Museo del Novecento, whose upper floors dedicate a large amount of space to the artist Lucio Fontana. It is here that one can see the luminous *Struttura al Neon per la IX Triennale di Milano*, a beautiful view especially when the sun sets; beyond the building's arches it resembles an arabesque of fluorescent light (below). Not far from it (opposite, top right) is *Soffitto Spaziale*, which the artist made for a hotel on Elba Island. The Museo del Novecento is among Milan's must-see sites because it celebrates the twentieth- and twenty-first century arts with masterpieces ranging from ones by Boccioni, Balla, Carrà, De Chirico, and Morandi, all the way to the most recent periods, represented by Nanda Vigo, Jannis Kounellis, and Mimmo Paladino.

900
MUSEO DEL
NOVECENTO

FUTUR
LIBER
TY
AVANGUARDIA E STILE
900 MUSEO DEL NOVECENTO

The last building that Gio Ponti built in Milan in the mid-1960s owes its name to the company that used it as its headquarters. An undisputed leading figure in Milanese culture, an architect, artist, the founder of the magazine *Domus*, the designer of ageless furniture, here Ponti expressed his innovative spirit: he chose ceramic cladding made up of four different types of tiles—three of which are in relief, to sculptural effect—and designed a series of windows with continuous variations. As he stated: "Architecture is made to be looked at. The facades are the walls of the streets."

PALAZZO MONTEDORIA

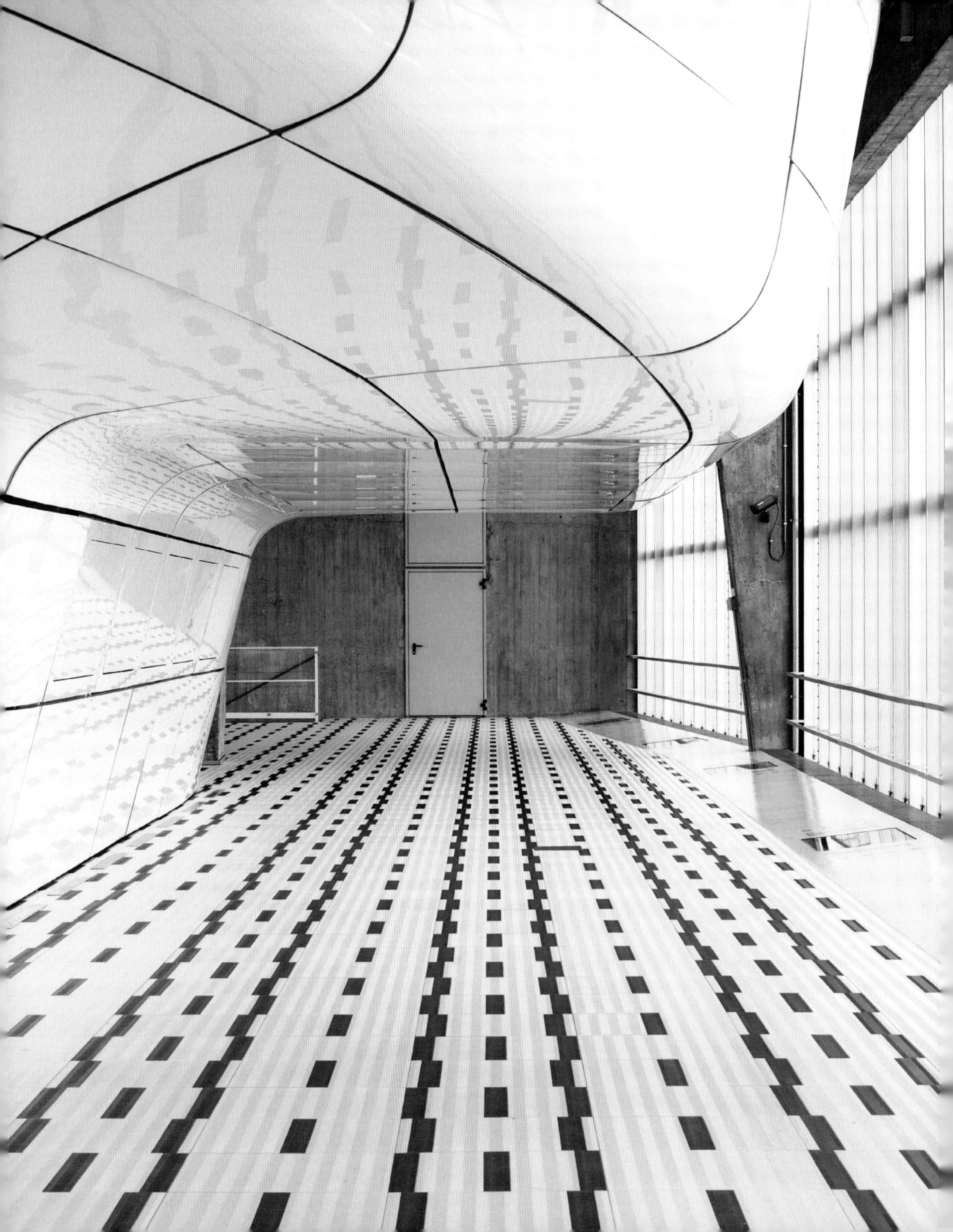

GRATTACIELO PIRELLI

Whereas the Duomo symbolizes historical Milan, the "Pirellone," as it is fondly called by the Milanese, is the image of modernity. Dating back to the 1960s, it was one of Europe's first high-rises: 416 feet tall, the expression of elegant rationality, it is Gio Ponti's masterpiece, with the consultancy of Pier Luigi Nervi, a structural engineer. Opposite, the belvedere on the 31st floor.

TORRE VELASCA

An architectural masterpiece, built between 1956 and 1958 by the BBPR firm. The expression of the contemporary, it is distinguished from other major buildings that were constructed in Milan at the time for its ties with structures of the past, in particular the Torre del Filarete of the Castello Sforzesco. Living in Torre Velasca has always been a mark of distinction, even though the building struggled at first to find consensus, both in the academic world and among the citizens.

TORRE SNIA VISCOSA

The first high-rise in Milan (1935–1937), romantically referred to at the time as "rubanuvole" (cloud-snatcher), expresses a twentieth-century language that characterizes many parts of the city. It rises up on the edge of Piazza San Babila, a crossroads that has become symbolic due to the urban changes that have made it a point of convergence between major roadways: Corso Vittorio Emanuele, Corso Europa, Corso Venezia, and Corso Matteotti, where Via Montenapoleone begins.

The square, with its ample size, is the result of the demolition of numerous previous constructions.
The location of houses and the offices of the chemical company Snia Viscosa, the eponymous tower is the work of Alessandro Rimini, a Jewish architect and painter.
Rimini lived a very difficult life, due to the race laws that were passed in 1938, but he never stopped working, designing numerous movie theaters as well as various buildings in the city.

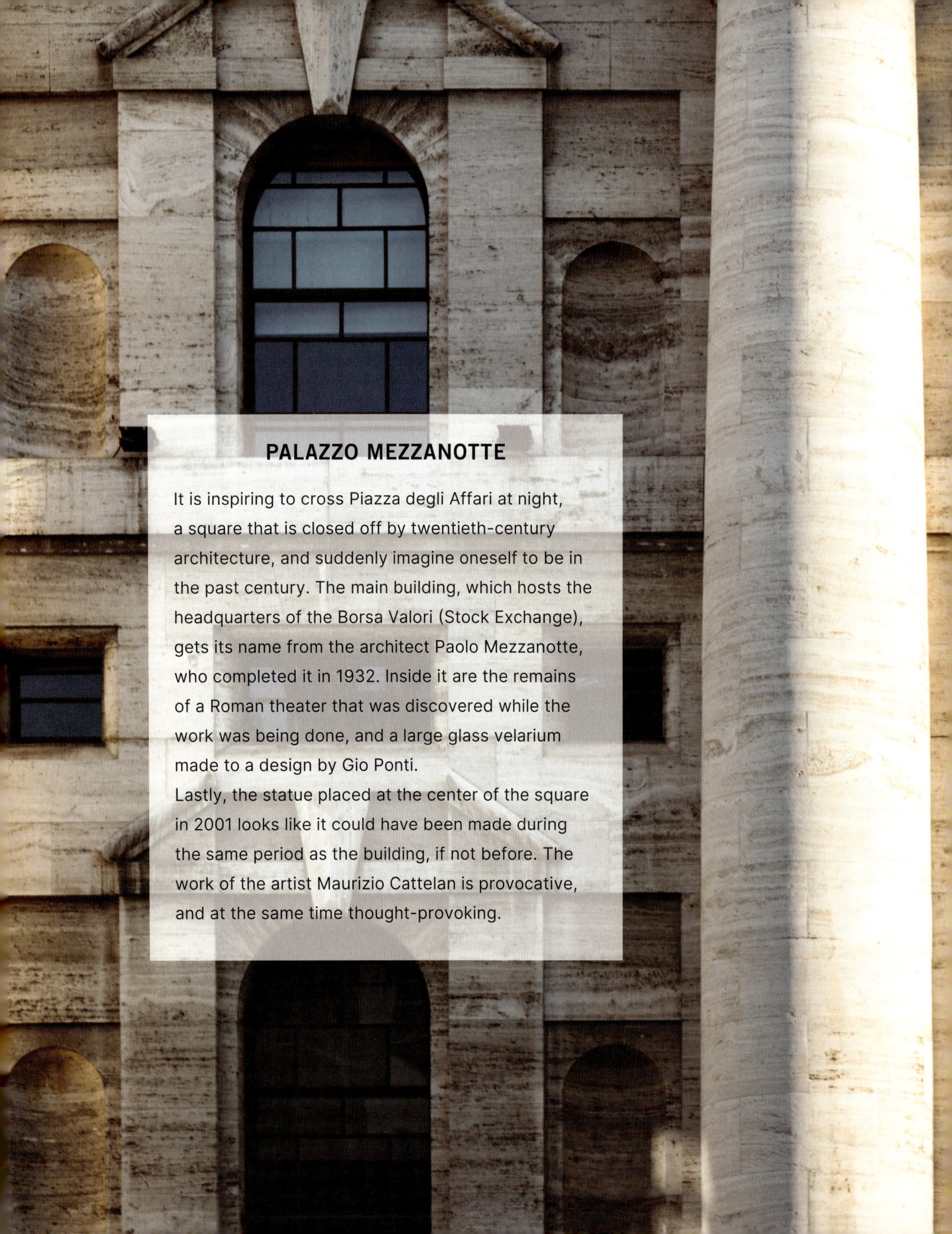

PALAZZO MEZZANOTTE

It is inspiring to cross Piazza degli Affari at night, a square that is closed off by twentieth-century architecture, and suddenly imagine oneself to be in the past century. The main building, which hosts the headquarters of the Borsa Valori (Stock Exchange), gets its name from the architect Paolo Mezzanotte, who completed it in 1932. Inside it are the remains of a Roman theater that was discovered while the work was being done, and a large glass velarium made to a design by Gio Ponti.
Lastly, the statue placed at the center of the square in 2001 looks like it could have been made during the same period as the building, if not before. The work of the artist Maurizio Cattelan is provocative, and at the same time thought-provoking.

ARMANI/SILOS
TRIENNALE MILANO
ADI DESIGN MUSEUM

Fashion and Design

When people talk about Milan's "Fashion Quadrilateral" they are referring to the area around Via Montenapoleone and the nearby streets, where the window displays of Italian designers and international brands follow one another in quick succession. It is an elegant shopping center where one can take a stroll, shop, or simply dream. Because Milanese fashion, ever since the first fashion shows of the 1970s to the present day, has never stopped creating dreams, thanks to the synergy between clever designers, talented photographers, and beautiful models. Behind these dreams lies a vast industry with impressive numbers and important revenues.

An undisputed leading figure, who has successfully combined entrepreneurship and creativity, is Giorgio Armani, or "King Giorgio." An acknowledged "Maestro," he has infused his work with a timeless sense of authority, promoting a vision of femininity that is soft and rigorous at the same time. To celebrate his style,

he created Armani/Silos, a vast space that used to be a grain storage facility and now serves to showcase his work, retracing a professional journey marked by its unique character.

Design has found its home in the Palazzo della Triennale. Since 1933, this building, located at the edge of Parco Sempione, has documented the evolution of living spaces, the creativity of a field that has made Milan famous, and the global reach of a discipline that thrives on the perfect fusion between craftsmanship and industry. Design, anti-design, and radical design have all passed through this space, interweaving with architecture, urban planning, photography, and the applied arts. From the 1960s onward, the relationship between designers and industry has developed in remarkable ways through experimentation, research, and collaborations. This has given rise to furniture pieces now considered classics and displayed in museums around the world. From functional objects to sculptural pieces that share the language of art, from innovative materials to the rediscovery of ancient techniques, there is a great deal that has found its place in the vast halls of this Palazzo, which over the years has produced many important cultural events.

The opening of the ADI Design Museum in 2021, inside an industrial building, celebrated the best projects that, since 1954, have been awarded the Compasso d'Oro. Gio Ponti invented the award, and the Associazione per il Design Industriale promoted it every two years. Hence the birth of a collection filled with 2,300 products and projects now on public display, so that viewers can admire it while reviewing a shared, ample, and complex story, perfectly summed up by the famous expression "from a spoon to a city."

ARMANI/SILOS

A warehouse from the 1950s, originally used to store grain, has become a container of elegance and beauty. By creating a space celebrating his long career, Giorgio Armani has given the city not just proof of his work, but also a vision of fashion, which, with an interdisciplinary slant, is connected to fine craftsmanship, art, cinema, and the aesthetic of the journey. “I decided to call it Silos,” the fashion designer remarked, “because that was where grain, food needed for survival, was stored. And, akin to food, wearing clothes is also necessary to survive.”

Armani was personally involved in the project to convert the 48,000 square feet that are spread over four levels. Rigor, monumentality, and modulated light create an exhibition theater that turns clothing, for men and for women, into genuine protagonists, divided into the themes that describe the worlds that inspired the stylist’s imagination.
On the top floor, an extensive digital archive available to the public includes the history of around 1,000 creations, with numerous photos, sketches, videos, and interviews.

On page 178, the staircase connecting the four levels allows the viewer to perceive the building's verticality.

Below, a corner of the section dedicated to menswear. Opposite, the entrance with the striking luminous facade of the foyer. The ground floor and the first floor are used for temporary exhibitions.

A L D O F A L L A I

Giorgio Armani's fondness for rigorous spaces, revealed in the chromatic contrast between the light hues and the black, mitigated by the gray of the concrete floor, is clear to see as one enters.

TRIENNALE MILANO

Since it was conceived, the Palazzo dell'Arte—designed by Giovanni Muzio in 1931 and opened to the public in 1933—has hosted the International Expositions of Decoration, and it continues to offer, every three years, an exhibition event that reflects on the contemporary in various disciplines. Featuring an imposing volume that was typical during the twenty-year rule of fascism, the building has proven just how flexible it is by hosting exhibitions, meetings, representations, and, since 2001, the Museo del Design, dedicated to Italian design and interpreting its many aspects via installations that differ each year. More recently, Cuore opened; it is a research center that has made the exhaustive number of documents held by the Triennale available to the public: over 300,000 works including objects, drawings, photographs, films, and archives. It also deserves credit for honoring the architectural space, celebrating Muzio's spiral staircase, which can now be viewed from the entrance hall.

On page 184 and opposite, Cuore – Research, study, and archives center, a space designed by Studio AR.CH.IT Luca Cipelletti, gives access to the various sections of the archive. On page 185, a detail of the original mosaic of the atrium floor. Above, a view of the 2024–2025 exhibition *Forme Mobili*, held at the Museo del Design Italiano, directed and curated by Marco Sammicheli, and designed by Luca Stoppini.

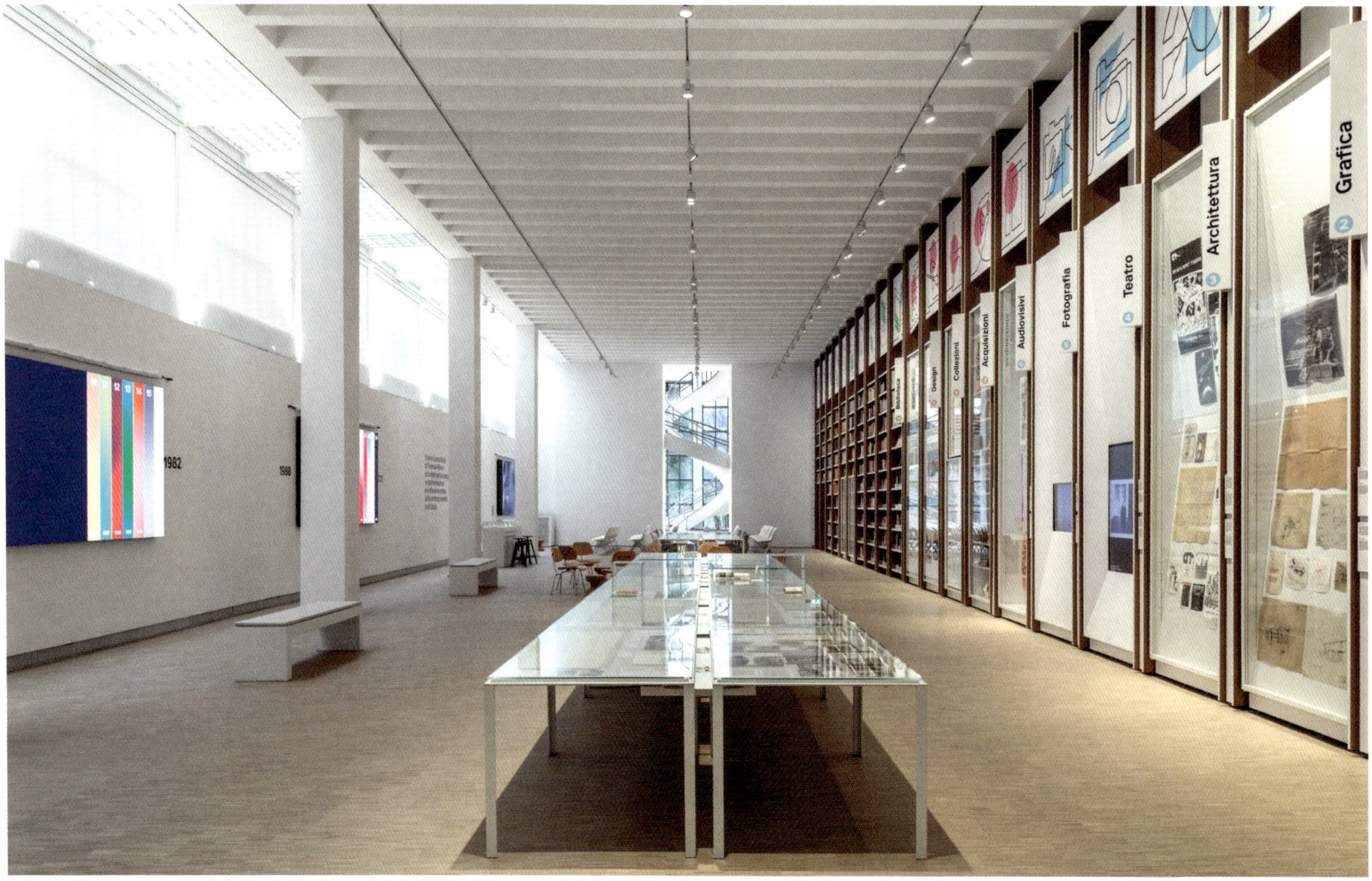
1982
1988
Grafica
Architettura
Teatro
Fotografia
Audiovisivi
Acquisizioni
Collezioni
Design

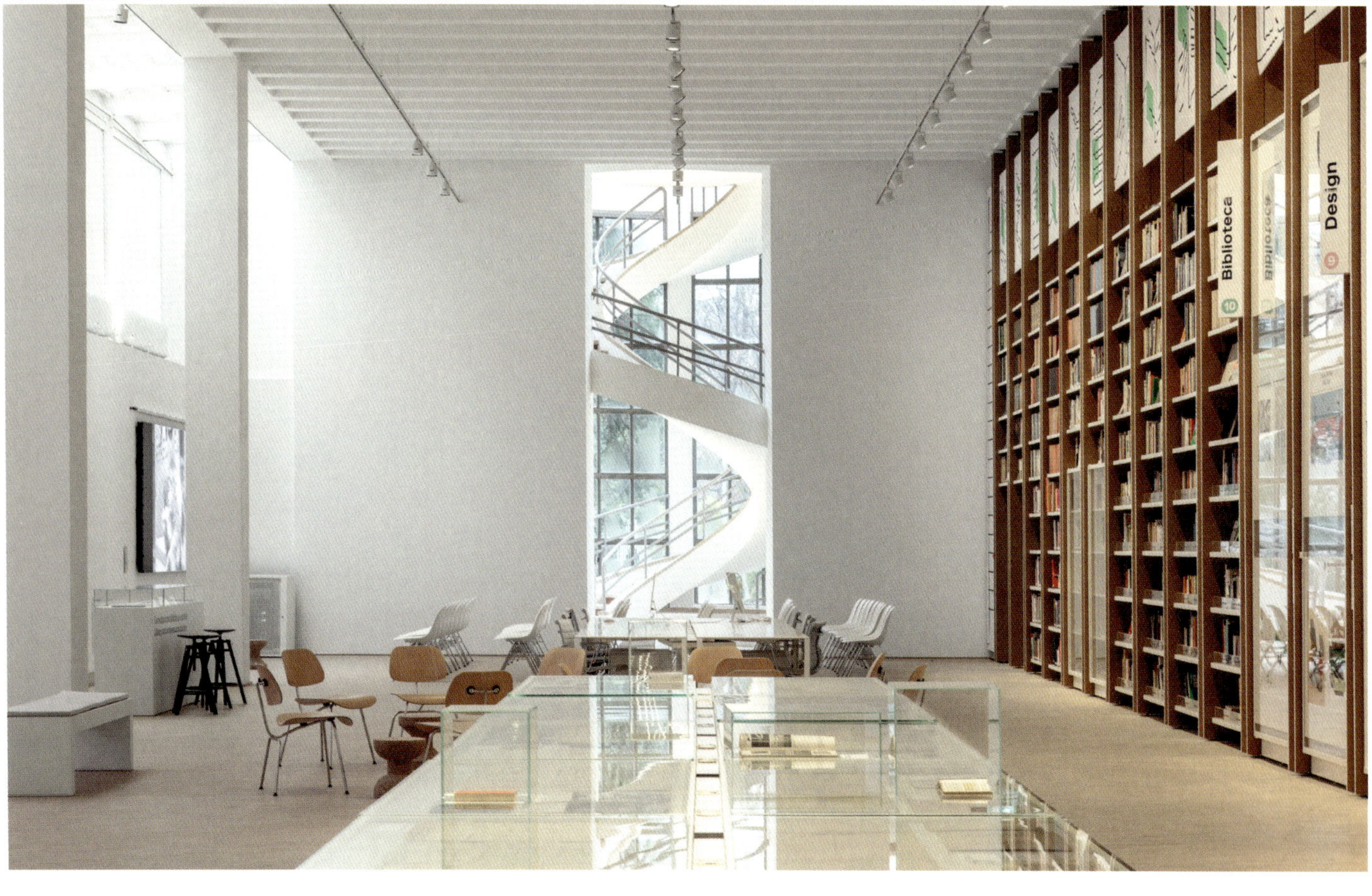
Biblioteca
Design

Opposite, at the back, Giovanni Muzio's spiral staircase, and, in the foreground, the long tables used for consulting in the Cuore area, whose walls display archive materials.
Below, the architectural model *Building for Bayer*, 1983, by Vittorio Gregotti, displayed in one of the showcases.
At bottom, details of the *Forme Mobili* exhibition, conceived as an invitation to think of movement as a design action.
On the following pages, looking upward at the entrance of the Palazzo dell'Arte.

Chapter.04

ADI DESIGN MUSEUM

From the second half of the twentieth century, ADI, Associazione per il Disegno Industriale, has played a crucial role in creating a community around the theme of Italian design, bringing together designers, companies, critics, and teachers. Under its curatorship, the prestigious Compasso d'Oro was created. Every two years, a jury of experts selects the best projects. The award is divided into numerous sections, not only related to lifestyle but extended to various other areas as well, including work, materials, mobility, and communication.

The copious holdings of the Compasso d'Oro have led to the creation of a very interesting collection, which is currently fittingly housed in the ADI Design Museum. It is framed by a building that was once a streetcar depot and a plant for the distribution of electric energy, whose glass front (pictured above) overlooks a recently opened garden-piazza. The museum has both permanent displays and temporary exhibitions, which have different themes addressed to the public at large as well as the specialists.

Interlude .01

On page 192 and opposite, top, are images of the temporary show *Best of Both Worlds: ITALY. Arte e Design in Italia 1915–2025*, which displays the timeless pieces made by the great masters; opposite, bottom, the exhibition *Fotografia alla Carriera*, a gallery of posters by major contemporary photographers dedicated to the winners of the Compasso d'Oro Career Award. Below, the 1964–1965 prize-winning projects in a section of the permanent collection.

RISTORANTE TORRE
IL BARETTO
FOUR SEASONS HOTEL

Lessons in Style

Luxury is expressed in many ways. The desire to store and elevate what tradition has to offer, or, on the contrary, the search for new expressions and experimentations both contribute to it. Over the years, Milan has managed to balance both paths with successful results. The world that was born around the Fondazione Prada looked beyond the solutions that were already known of, commissioning an architect of the caliber of Rem Koolhaas, who called the genesis of the restaurant-bar on top of the Torre "a collage of themes and preexisting elements." Nonetheless, Koolhaas managed to bestow a contemporary mark on the place as a whole. The Ristorante Torre, on the higher floor of a building that has elements of boldness, comes into view from a panoramic glass elevator. Retrofuturism has been mentioned, a term that encapsulates the double movement: that looking back, to the esprit

of the 1950s, by way of the furnishings and the works of art, to then design a future just as we imagined it to be. The result of this is a place that makes its guests feel good, which is no small thing.
Quite different is the setting of the Four Seasons Hotel Milano, in an ancient monastery. A project that during the construction phase had to deal with a number of surprises, revealed as the work to tear down obsolete structures progressed: to name one, the emergence of ancient columns in the Renaissance cloister that had been erased by eighteenth-century interventions.
The conservative method used respected the frescoes, the Late Middle Age vaults, the patrician fireplace, reconciling between them the layers of history, from the Middle Ages to the present, with its inescapable needs. A full immersion in the past accompanied by the most sophisticated comforts of modern times.

RISTORANTE TORRE

Art, haute cuisine, a panoramic view of the city from the terrace. This too: important elements from a historical restaurant like the Four Seasons Hotel Milano, born in 1958 in New York, designer furniture, and ceramic works by Lucio Fontana. The projects designed by Prada with the collaboration of Rem Koolhaas (here with Chris van Duijn and Federico Pompignoli from OMA studio) are born from a number of realities combined in multidisciplinary designs.

The result, in this case, is a space on the sixth floor of the Torre, the last piece of the Fondazione that develops opposite a large glass pane opening onto an external terrace. The modernity lies in the food, which experiments without being too extreme, while the space assembles elements of significant artistic and architectural moments and creates, at several levels that are slightly staggered, a setting that is softened by the wooden floors, the walnut boiserie, and the hemp panels covering the walls.
There is a sense of refined hospitality in the air: one has lunch before the city skyline, while dinner is accompanied by the view of the lights and the reflections on the windows.
There are three works by Fontana: *Pilastro*, 1947 (in detail on the previous pages), that marks the passage between the bar area and the restaurant, preceded, in the area around the Soviet chairs by Eero Saarinen, by *Cappa per caminetto*, 1949, and *Testa di Medusa*, 1948–1954. In the upper part of the restaurant, the furnishings from the Four Seasons in New York coexist with elements from the installation by Carsten Höller, *The Double Club*, 2008–2009. In accordance with Italian tradition, a series of artist's plates hang on the wall.

Two magnificent works by Lucio Fontana, *Cappa per caminetto*, 1949 and *Testa di Medusa*, 1948–1954; chairs and tables designed by Eero Saarinen.

IL BARETTO

British atmosphere and Milanese tradition merge in one of the most famous restaurants right in the heart of the city. An old-fashioned club that combines tartan-patterned carpeting and dark boiserie with windows facing the greenery outdoors—a place where guests can relax at the table, far from the noise of the traffic. Both Milanese and tourists can savor dishes that range from seafood (above is the Catalan-style lobster) to the more traditional *cotoletta alla milanese* (breaded veal cutlet). The food is notable for the high quality of the ingredients used.

FOUR SEASONS HOTEL

Offered here is the peacefulness that once characterized the convent of the Poor Clares, who lived here in the fifteenth century, and at the same time the grandeur of a noble palazzo, which is what it was in the second half of the eighteenth century for the Marchesi D'Adda. The Four Seasons Hotel Milano boasts a location of considerable historical value, which preserves significant traces of its past: the large sandstone fireplace (previous pages), whose architrave features the coat of arms of the D'Adda, in the lounge on the ground floor; the vaults of the porch, also present in some of the rooms; and the major frescoes of the ancient church of the monastery. A volume that hosts a combination of one hundred eighteen rooms and suites, a roomy cloister that can be enjoyed during a drink or lunch on the veranda, and the restaurant Zelo, opposite.

From the left, a corner of the lounge on the ground floor, the hallways that open onto the cloister, a green oasis, and the ancient columns.

MILAN, TO READ AND TO WATCH

MILANESE STORIES

Luciano Bianciardi, *It's a Hard Life*. New York: Viking Press, 1965 [1962].

Dino Buzzati, *A Love Affair*. New York: NYRB, 2023 [1963].

Giorgio Scerbanenco, *A Private Venus*. Abingdon (UK): Hersilia Press, 2012 [1966].

Umberto Eco, *Numero Zero*. New York: HarperVia, 2016.

MILAN IN VERSE

Giovanni Raboni, *Selected Poems*. New York: Gradiva Publications, 2001.

Franco Loi, *Air and Memory*. Denver (CO): Counterpath Press, 2008 [2005].

Alda Merini, *Love Lessons: Selected Poems of Alda Merini*. Princeton (NJ): Princeton University Press, 2016.

ITINERARIES AND ESSAYS

John Foot, *Milan since the Miracle*. Oxford and New York: Berg Publishers, 2001.

Massimo Polidoro, *Secret Milan*. Versailles: Jonglez Publishing, 2015 [2012].

Giulia Castelli Gattinara, *111 Places in Milan That You Must Not Miss*. Cologne: Emons Publishers, 2015.

Carlo Berizzi, *Milan. Architectural Guide*. Berlin: DOM Publishers, 2019.

Marco Biraghi and Adriana Granato, *The Architecture of Milan: The City Written by Architects From the Post-War Period to Today*. Milan: Hoepli Editore, 2021.

Jada Bai, et al., *The Passenger. Milan: For Explorers of the World*. Milan: Iperborea, 2022.

Silvia Frau, *The 500 Hidden Secrets of Milan*. Antwerp: Luster Publishing, 2022.

ILLUSTRATED BOOKS

Karl Kolbitz (ed.), *Entryways of Milan*. Cologne: Taschen 2017.

Lisa Licitra Ponti, *Gio Ponti and Milan. A Guide to the Works 1920–1970*. Rome: Quodlibet, 2018.

Carlo Orsi and Aldo Nove, *Milano*. Milan: Skira, 2019.

Marco Sammicheli and Anna Mainoli, *The Design City. Milan: Extraordinary Lab*. Florence: Forma, 2019 [2018].

Patrizia Piccinini, *Piero Portaluppi. Between Tradition and the Avant-garde*. New York: Rizzoli, 2022 [2021].

Castellini Baldissera with photography by Guido Taroni, *Inside Milan*. New York and London: Vendôme Press, 2022.

Enrico Morteo and Orsina Simona Pierini, *Nelle case/Milan interiors. 1928–1978*. Milan: Hoepli, 2023.

MILAN IN FILM

Vittorio De Sica, *Miracolo a Milano* (*Miracle in Milan*), 1951.

Luchino Visconti, *Rocco e i suoi fratelli* (*Rocco and His Brothers*), 1960.

Michelangelo Antonioni, *La notte* (*The Night*), 1961.

Mario Monicelli, *Renzo e Luciana, an Episode of Boccaccio '70*, 1962.

Carlo Lizzani, *Banditi a Milano* (*Bandits in Milan*), 1968.

Castellano & Pipolo, *Il ragazzo di campagna* (*The Country Boy*) 1984.

Silvio Soldini, *Un'anima divisa in due* (*A Soul Split in Two*), 1993.

Luca Guadagnino, *Io sono l'amore* (*I Am Love*), 2009.

Ridley Scott, *The House of Gucci,* 2021.

Roan Johnson, *Monterossi*, TV series, 2022, 2023.

Gabriele Salvatores*, Il ritorno di Casanova* (*Casanova's Return*), 2023.

Andrea Di Stefano*, Ultima notte d'amore* (*Last Night of Amore*), 2023.

INDEX OF PLACES

Page numbers refer to images

Front cover
A view of the Indro Montanelli Gardens
and the Museum of Natural History from the terrace
of Casa Cipriani.
In the background, the Porta Nuova neighborhood.

Photographs
© 2025 Lea Anouchinsky

Editorial Project Manager
Valentina Lindon

Art Direction and Graphic Design
Teikna Design / Claudia Neri and Elisa Stagnoli

Translation
Sylvia Adrian Notini

Distributed in English throughout the World by
Rizzoli International Publications, Inc.
49 West 27th Street
New York, NY 10001
www.rizzoliusa.com

ISBN: 978-88-918-4425-5

Printed in Italy
2025 2026 2027 2028 / 10 9 8 7 6 5 4 3 2 1

The authorized representative in the EU for safety and compliance is Mondadori Libri S.p.A.,
via Gian Battista Vico 42, Milan, Italy, 20123
http://www.mondadori.it

Photo Credits

p. 100: Courtesy of the artist and Pirelli HangarBicocca

p. 101: Courtesy Fondazione Fausto Melotti and Pirelli HangarBicocca
© Fausto Melotti, by SIAE 2025

pp. 160–161: Lucio Fontana, *Struttura al neon per la IX Triennale di Milano. Neon spaziale,* 1951 (2010), Milan, Museo del Novecento
© Fondazione Lucio Fontana, Milano, by SIAE 2025

pp. 200–201: Lucio Fontana, *Pilastro*, 1957, Fondazione Prada, Milan, Ristorante Torre
© Fondazione Lucio Fontana, Milano, by SIAE 2025

p. 202: Carsten Höller, *The double club*, part of an interior installation, 2008–2009, Fondazione Prada, Milan, Ristorante Torre © Carsten Höller, by SIAE

p. 204: Lucio Fontana, *Testa di Medusa*, 1948–1954, Fondazione Prada, Milan, Ristorante Torre
© Fondazione Lucio Fontana, Milano, by SIAE 2025

pp. 204–205: Lucio Fontana, *Cappa per caminetto*, 1949, Fondazione Prada, Milan, Ristorante Torre
© Fondazione Lucio Fontana, Milano, by SIAE 2025

Triennale Milano

pp. 184, 187, 188: view of Giovanni Muzio's spiral staircase inside Cuore – Research, study, and archives center, at Triennale Milano
p. 185: Leonor Fini (cartoon by Achille Funi), *Cavalcade of Amazons*, 1933
p. 186: *Forme Mobili*, installation of the Museo del Design Italiano at Triennale, Milano: Antonio Citterio, *Divano Max*, 1983, Flexform (2023); Anna Castelli Ferrieri, *Sedie impilabili* mod. 4870, 1983, Kartell (1985); Jac Jacobsen/Naska Loris Lux Italia, *Naska Loris Gigante*, 1983, Naska Loris Lux; Gio Ponti, *Superleggera (o mod. 699)*, 1955, Cassina (1957); Cinzia Ruggeri, *Cane Pipì*, 1999, Flexform advertising campaign 1984. Photo Gabriele Basilico/Archivio Gabriele Basilico
p. 189: top, Vittorio Gregotti, *Building for Bayer*, architectural model (model by Giovanni Sacchi), 1983, Collezione Giovanni Sacchi della Regione Lombardia – Triennale Milano; AG Fronzoni, *Serie 64*, 1964, Galli (1964), Cappellini (1997); bottom left, Enzo Mari, *Serie Elementare* tiles, 1968, Gabbianelli (1972); Roberto Gabetti, Aimaro Isola, Luciano Re, Guido Drocco, *Tapipardo* carpet (*Tapizoo* series), 1970, Paracchi/ARBO (1970), Amini (2023, at the initiative of Lodovico Gabetti and Fabrizio Pellegrino); bottom right, furniture for Osvaldo Borsani. Carlo Mollino, *Arabesco*, 1949, Apelli&Varesio (1950), Zanotta (1997) and Carlo Mollino, *Mobile divisorio* per casa *Albonico*, 1944, Apelli&Varesio, Comodato Direzione Regionale Musei Lombardia, Triennale Milano

Visit us online:
Instagram.com/RizzoliBooks
Facebook.com/RizzoliNewYork
Youtube.com/user/RizzoliNY